WATER /
WASTEWATER
ENGINEER

NEL YOMTOV

Published in the United States of America by Cherry Lake Publishing
Ann Arbor, Michigan
www.cherrylakepublishing.com

Content Adviser: Jennifer McElroy, PE, Senior Environmental Engineer, Water/Wastewater Engineering, Gainesville Regional Utilities, Gainesville, FL
Reading Adviser: Marla Conn, ReadAbility, Inc.

Photo Credits: ©GRU (Gainesville Regional Utilities) and Cheuvront Studios, cover, 1, 6, 9, 17, 21, 22, 26; ©Jitinatt Jufask/Shutterstock Images, 5; ©CharlesOstrand/Shutterstock Images, 11; ©MarArt/Shutterstock Images, 12; ©supakiat/Shutterstock Images, 14; ©Blend Images/Shutterstock Images, 15; ©Jonutis/Shutterstock Images, 18; ©Goodluz/Shutterstock Images, 25, 29

Library of Congress Cataloging-in-Publication Data

Yomtov, Nelson, author.
Water/Wastewater Engineer / Nel Yomtov.
     pages cm. — (Cool STEAM careers)
  Summary: "Readers will learn what it takes to succeed as a wastewater engineer. The book also explains the necessary educational steps, useful character traits, and daily job tasks related to this career, in the framework of the STEAM (Science, Technology, Engineering, Art, and Math) movement. Photos, a glossary, and additional resources are included."— Provided by publisher.
  Audience: Ages 8-12.
  Audience: Grades 4 to 6.
  Includes bibliographical references and index.
  ISBN 978-1-63362-010-0 (hardcover) — ISBN 978-1-63362-049-0 (pbk.) — ISBN 978-1-63362-088-9 (pdf) — ISBN 978-1-63362-127-5 (ebook) 1. Water—Purification—Juvenile literature. 2. Sewage—Purification—Juvenile literature. 3. Water-supply engineering—Vocational guidance—Juvenile literature. 4. Water treatment plants—Management—Juvenile literature. I. Title.

  TD430.Y66 2015
  628.1—dc23   2014031418

Cherry Lake Publishing would like to acknowledge the work of
The Partnership for 21st Century Skills. Please visit www.p21.org
for more information.

Printed in the United States of America
Corporate Graphics

ABOUT THE AUTHOR

Nel Yomtov is an award-winning author of nonfiction books and graphic novels for young readers. He lives in the New York City area.

TABLE OF CONTENTS

STEAM is the acronym for Science, Technology, Engineering, Arts, and Mathematics. In this book, you will read about how each of these study areas is connected to a career in water/wastewater engineering.

CHAPTER 1

WATER: THE LIFEBLOOD OF EARTH

Annie and her father had just finished cleaning the fish tank. She slowly poured the dirty water into the laundry room sink. She seemed puzzled as she watched the water swirl down the drain. "Dad, what happens to the water we use? Where does it go?" she asked.

"You mean the water we use after taking a shower or using the toilet? Or even this dirty water from the fish tank?" he asked.

"Right. Or when the dishwasher runs," she replied.

"The water we use has to be cleaned. Then it is

returned to places in the environment like rivers."

"Cleaned?" she asked in disbelief. "Who cleans our water?"

"The people who clean and recycle dirty water are called water/wastewater **engineers**," he said.

"What a great job," Annie replied. "And an important one, too! I'd sure like to be a water/wastewater engineer!"

Water that goes down the drain is later cleaned and returned to the environment.

Water/wastewater engineers inspect facilities to make sure all processes run smoothly.

Water/wastewater engineering is the science of supplying fresh, clean water to people, homes, and businesses, and treating and disposing of **wastewater**. Wastewater is any kind of water that has been used in some way that affects the quality of the water—such as bathing, washing clothes, or using the toilet. It can come from homes, offices, businesses, manufacturing plants, and even farms. Wastewater can contain **bacteria**, chemicals, **pollutants**, and wastes that are harmful to people, wildlife, and the environment.

THINK ABOUT SCIENCE

Water/wastewater engineers use a variety of sciences to treat wastewater before the water is returned to the environment. Wastewater treatment uses physical, biological, and chemical processes to remove waste and harmful pollutants. If you are interested in a career in water management, plan on taking courses in biology, physics, chemistry, and environmental sciences.

Environmental or civil engineers with special training in water/wastewater are called water/wastewater engineers. They play an important role in keeping our communities healthy, while providing us with safe drinking water. These skilled and well-trained professionals are involved in a wide variety of tasks and programs. Among them are designing and maintaining water and wastewater treatment systems and water storage facilities, such as **reservoirs**. Water/wastewater engineers must consider many factors when designing these structures, including construction costs and government regulations. They must also conduct research to study the **impact** of their water supply and water treatment systems on the environment.

All this talk about water may be making you thirsty. But before you reach for a refreshing glass of the wet stuff, let's take a look at some water basics. You might be surprised at what you discover!

Engineers and a water plant operator review treatment facility plans together to modify and maintain the framework.

WATER BASICS

Did you know that Earth is covered by more than 326 million trillion gallons of water? And that about 71 percent of our planet is covered in ocean? Yet even with all this water, people can use only less than 1 percent of the water on Earth. The rest is salt water and water locked up in glaciers and the polar ice caps. We cannot drink it, wash with it, or use it to water plants or grow crops.

Water may be the most common substance on Earth's surface, but it is a limited resource. There will never be any more water on Earth than there is now. Scientists can create lots of amazing things, but they cannot create more water. The water in every drop of rain and every glass of water you drink might seem new, but it has always been here and always will be. Water's eternal life is called the **water cycle**.

Water is a limited resource.

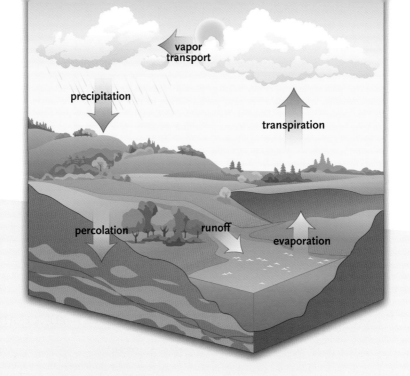

This illustration shows the water cycle.

Here's how the water cycle works. Heat from the sun causes water on Earth to **evaporate**, or turn from a liquid into a gas, and rise into the sky. The gas, or **water vapor**, gathers in the sky to form clouds. As the water vapor cools down, it becomes water again. The water falls from the sky in the form of rain, snow, or sleet. This process is called **precipitation**. Oceans, rivers, and lakes collect the water that has fallen. Water that falls onto the ground seeps into the earth and eventually drains into these bodies of water or to an aquifer. An aquifer is an underground layer of rock, sand, or gravel that is filled with water. Valuable drinking water is pumped from aquifers.

As the world's population grows, millions and millions more people need water, a precious, life-giving but limited resource. Therefore, it's especially important that we use our water wisely and not waste it.

THINK ABOUT TECHNOLOGY

Water/wastewater engineers use cutting-edge technologies to keep our planet healthy. For example, high-tech research tools help engineers collect and analyze data and conduct water quality studies. Water/wastewater engineers also use computer software to design treatment plants, water storage tanks, and pumping systems. Examples of this type of technology include computer-aided design (CAD) and geographic information systems (GIS).

You may have seen a water tower like this. They are built in all shapes and sizes and painted with a wide variety of colors.

Have you ever wondered where the water comes from when you turn on a tap in your home? Most people living in the United States get their water from surface water, such as lakes or rivers, or from aquifers. About 85 percent of all Americans get their water from public water supply systems. In more rural areas, people often get their water from private underground wells.

Where you get your water may depend on whether you live near a large city or in a rural area.

Keeping it Clean

The main job of a water reclamation facility designed by water/wastewater engineers is to make wastewater clean enough to be sent back into the environment. All the bacteria, chemicals, and other pollutants must be removed or brought down to acceptable levels before this can be done. In general, engineers design two types of wastewater treatment systems: biological treatment plants and physical-chemical treatment plants.

Biological treatment plants use bacteria to break down waste. Generally, the solid wastes are separated

Engineers pay close attention to the health of the microorganisms living in this basin to ensure the treatment process runs efficiently.

from the water using a piece of equipment called a bar screen. A bar screen looks similar to a large rake on a chain. Grit, or very small solids, is also removed. The remaining water is then sent to a basin. Most basins are rectangular. There, the wastewater is mixed with **microorganisms**, which break down the nutrients left in the water. Water/wastewater engineers often refer to these microorganisms as "bugs."

After treatment with the bacteria, the water is filtered and treated with a chemical called a **disinfectant**.

In this clarifier, solids settle to the bottom and clear
water pours off the top to be treated further.

Treating wastewater removes dangerous materials such as human and animal waste, chemicals, and disease-causing viruses and bacteria from the water. When the treated water is sent back into the environment, it is safe for the fish and wildlife that depend on it.

Designing wastewater treatment plants is an important part of a water/wastewater engineer's job, but it's certainly not the only one. Let's take a closer look at the other duties performed by these protectors of our water supply.

THINK ABOUT ENGINEERING

Water/wastewater engineering is part of the broader field called civil engineering. Civil engineers design, build, and maintain structures such as treatment plants, reservoirs, bridges and roads, pipelines, and dams. Environmental engineers are trained in water and wastewater management, air pollution control, and solid waste management. Their job is to protect and improve the natural environment. Most water/wastewater engineers have degrees in civil or environmental engineering.

CHAPTER 4

WATER/WASTEWATER ENGINEERS AT WORK

Water/wastewater engineers perform a wide variety of duties. Among their many responsibilities are:

- Designing water and wastewater treatment plants, pumping systems, and other systems and networks for drinkable and nondrinkable water

- Analyzing and recommending **sludge** treatment and disposal

- Conducting environmental impact studies related to water and wastewater treatment and distribution

*Although engineers create **models** and plans on computers, they have to visit sites to make sure everything is working properly.*

- Studying water resources, such as streams and rivers, wetlands, and ocean coastlines
- Gathering and analyzing water-use information to predict water demand
- Writing reports and articles related to water resources and water-use efficiency
- Ensuring systems are designed and maintained to protect the environment
- Testing water quality

Engineers examine and verify the amount of chemicals added to an odor control system at a water reclamation, or recovery, facility.

Water/wastewater engineers perform their work in many settings. The most common are private utility companies, engineering firms, large industrial plants, and wastewater training organizations. Some water/wastewater engineers are self-employed, working mainly as consultants. About 40 percent of water/wastewater engineers in the United States work for local, state, or federal governments.

In 1972, the Clean Water Act was passed to eliminate sources of water pollution and develop standards for wastewater treatment. In 1974, the Safe Drinking Water Act was passed to protect the nation's drinking water. These acts provided work opportunities for many water/wastewater engineers.

Water and wastewater engineers often work outdoors and take a "hands-on" approach to oversee operations or solve on-site problems. Some travel to work sites across the United States and foreign countries. Many work with government officials to ensure that private and public water supply and wastewater facilities meet government standards and regulations.

THINK ABOUT ART

A background in art can enhance an engineer's ability to design structures, especially ones viewable by the public. Structures and buildings such as water treatment plants, water towers, water reclamation facilities, and pumping stations are designed to have visual appeal and blend in with the surrounding landscape.

CHAPTER 5

Becoming a Water/ Wastewater Engineer

Becoming a water/wastewater engineer requires planning, training, and education. It also helps to have the right personal skills and abilities. For entry-level positions, you will need at least a bachelor of engineering (BE) degree in civil, mechanical, chemical, or environmental engineering. Specialty courses might include laboratory analysis and water and wastewater treatment. BE programs also require courses in calculus and statistics, physics, computer science, English composition, and chemistry.

Earning a master's degree may require a class in environmental science.

Higher-level positions in water/wastewater careers often require a master's degree in engineering (ME). Courses in this master's program may include flood control, geology, water chemistry/biology, and environmental science and technology. Depending on the type of setting, water/wastewater engineers typically do not operate the plants. Plant operators, who have certification, are responsible for plant operations. These operators must pass a rigorous certification exam.

*Engineers use computers and other technology to model the
water/wastewater system and make improvements.*

Engineers work closely with operators to design water/
wastewater treatment facilities. They also work together to
solve any problems that arise. A good working relationship
between operators and engineers is important for a
successful treatment system.

Obtaining a college degree might be years away, but
it's not too early for future water/wastewater engineers
to get on the right career path. In high school, build a
solid background in mathematics that includes algebra,
geometry, trigonometry, and calculus. Take courses in

science, especially biology, chemistry, and physics. Study a foreign language, if courses are offered. Also, remember to take those all-important courses in English composition and computers, too.

The field of water/wastewater management is growing rapidly. Between 2010 and 2020, employment in the industry will have increased by more than 21 percent. This means lots of good job opportunities for the right

THINK ABOUT MATH

Water/wastewater engineers use the term model to refer to mathematical equations that represent sources of water, such as aquifers, rivers and streams, ocean coastlines, and floodplains. Mathematical relationships are used to predict, for example, water quantity, the rate of river or stream flows, and water quality. This information helps water/wastewater engineers develop plans for new water resources or water efficiency programs.

candidates. California, Florida, New York, Texas, and Massachusetts are the states that currently have the most water and wastewater engineers. Job growth is especially high in Vermont, Louisiana, and Connecticut.

According to the U.S. Bureau of Labor Statistics, the median salary of water/wastewater engineers in the United States is about $80,000. The median salary is the wage that half the workers earned more than and half earned less than. Canada's Environmental Careers Organization (ECO) reports that the average entry-level water/wastewater engineer position salary is roughly $40,000 per year.

Water and wastewater management can be a rewarding career. It takes years of education and hard work, but the job you do as a water/wastewater engineer helps people live healthier, safer lives and safeguards the environment. It is a well-respected and admired profession that is worth the effort.

Are you up for the challenge?

Some of the work water/wastewater engineers do is performed outdoors.

THINK ABOUT IT

After reading this book, what do you think makes a water/wastewater engineer's job important?

Look online or visit a library to find out what effects untreated wastewater has on the environment.

Review chapters 2 and 3 again. How do water/ wastewater engineers use science and technology to perform their jobs?

LEARN MORE

FURTHER READING

Fridell, Ron. *Protecting Earth's Water Supply*. Minneapolis: Lerner Publications, 2009.

Morgan, Sally. *Earth's Water Cycle*. Mankato, MN: Smart Apple Media, 2012.

Mulder, Michelle. *Every Last Drop: Bringing Clean Water Home*. Custer, WA: Orca Footprints, 2014.

WEB SITES

National Academy of Engineering—Engineer Girl
www.engineergirl.org
Explore a career in engineering by reading an interview with an engineer and find out how to enter an essay contest about how engineering impacts our world.

Science Buddies—Water or Wastewater Engineer
www.sciencebuddies.org/science-fair-projects/science-engineering-careers/
EnvEng_waterorwastewaterengineer_c001.shtml
Start your career in science by learning what water/wastewater engineers do and what qualifications are required.

United States Geological Survey—The USGS Water Science School
http://water.usgs.gov/edu
Get the facts on water basics, the water cycle, water quality, and what you can do to conserve Earth's water supply and keep it clean.

GLOSSARY

bacteria (bak-TEER-ee-uh) microscopic, single-celled living things that exist everywhere and can either be useful or harmful

disinfectant (dis-in-FEK-tuhnt) a chemical used to kill germs

engineers (en-juh-NEERZ) people who are specially trained to design, build, and maintain large machines, structures, or public works such as wastewater treatment plants

evaporate (i-VAP-uh-rate) to change into a vapor or gas

impact (IM-pakt) a strong impression something or someone has made on something or someone else

microorganisms (mye-kroh-OR-guh-niz-uhmz) organisms too small to be seen without a microscope, such as bacteria, rotifers, protozoans, and metazoans

model (MAH-dul) a mathematical equation that is used to represent situations, such as the quality of water or the flow rate of rivers and streams

pollutants (puh-LOO-tuhnts) substances that contaminate another substance

precipitation (pri-sip-i-TAY-shuhn) the falling of water from the sky in the form of rain, sleet, hail, or snow

reservoirs (REZ-ur-vwahrz) natural or artificial lakes in which water is collected and stored for use

sludge (SLUHJ) waste product that is a mixture of solids and liquid

wastewater (WAYST-waw-tur) water that has been used in some way that affects the quality of the water

water cycle (WAW-tur SYE-kul) the constant movement of Earth's water

water vapor (WAW-tur VAY-per) the gas state of water

INDEX